THE GREAT BOOK OF NIGERIA

AN EDUCATIONAL NIGERIA TRAVEL FACTS WITH PICTURE BOOK FOR KIDS ABOUT HISTORY, DESTINATION PLACES, ANIMALS, AND MANY MORE

Copyright @2024 James K. Mahi

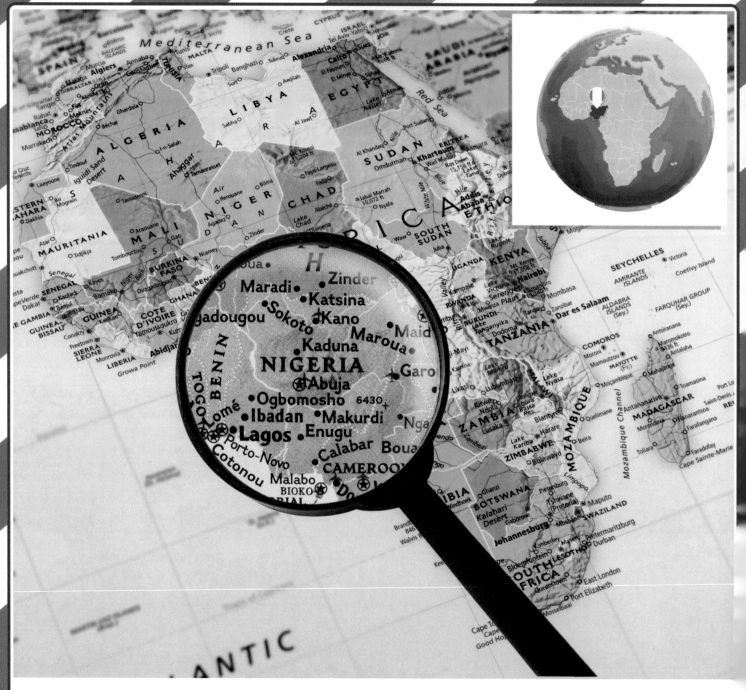

Nigeria is located in **West Africa** and is the most populous country on the continent.

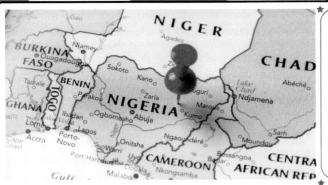

Which continent does Nigeria belong to?

Nigeria belongs to the continent of Africa.

How many countries does Nigeria border?

Nigeria borders four countries: Benin, Niger, Chad, and Cameroon.

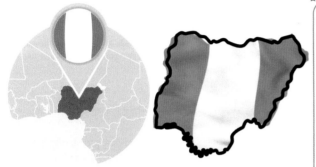

How big is Nigeria?

Nigeria covers an area of about 923,768 square kilometers.

What percentage of the world's land does Nigeria occupy?

Nigeria occupies about 0.3% of the world's land area.

What percentage of Nigeria is covered by rainforests?

Approximately 7% of Nigeria is covered by rainforests.

Which city is the largest in Nigeria?

The largest city in Nigeria is Lagos.

How many provinces does Nigeria have?

Nigeria is divided into 36 states and one Federal Capital Territory (Abuja).

What is the population of Nigeria?

The population of Nigeria is approximately 222.6 million people.

Is Nigeria overly populated?
Yes, Nigeria is considered to be one of the most populous countries in the world.
What are the people of Nigeria called?
The people of Nigeria are called Nigerians.

What is Nigeria's literacy rate?
Nigeria's literacy rate is around 59%.

Who ruled Nigeria first?
Nigeria was initially colonized and ruled by the British.

What is the national animal of Nigeria?
The national animal of Nigeria is the Eagle.

What is the national bird of Nigeria?
The national bird of Nigeria is the Black Crowned Crane.

The Federal Republic of Nigeria.

What is the official name of Nigeria?
The official name of Nigeria is the Federal Republic of Nigeria.
What is Nigeria's nickname?
Nigeria is often referred to as the "Giant of Africa".

The capital city of Nigeria is Abuja, but the largest city is Lagos.

Nigeria gained its independence from British rule on October 1, 1960.

The official language of Nigeria is English.

Nigeria is known for its diverse culture, with over 250 ethnic groups and 500 languages spoken.

The Nollywood film industry in Nigeria is the second-largest in the world, after Bollywood in India.

Nigeria is rich in natural resources, including oil, **which is a major contributor to its economy.**

Nigeria is home to the Yoruba, Igbo, and Hausa-Fulani **ethnic groups, among others.**

The Niger River, **one of Africa's longest rivers, flows through Nigeria.**

Nigeria has a tropical climate with a rainy season from April to October and a dry season from November to March.

Nigeria is known for its vibrant music scene, **producing famous musicians like Fela Kuti and Burna Boy.**

The national sport of Nigeria is soccer, and the country has a strong presence in international competitions.

Nigeria is home to a variety of wildlife, including elephants, lions, and endangered species like the Cross River gorilla.

The Naira **is the official currency of Nigeria.**

Nigeria is the sixth-most populous country in the world, **with over 222 million people.**

The Zuma Rock, located near Abuja, is a famous natural landmark in Nigeria.

Nigeria has a diverse range of traditional cuisines, including jollof rice, suya, and egusi soup.

The Ogbunike Caves in Anambra State are a UNESCO World Heritage Site and hold cultural significance.

The National Mosque in Abuja and the National Christian Centre are important religious landmarks in Nigeria.

Aso Rock, a 400-meter tall monolith, is the most noticeable feature in the capital city, Abuja.

Nigeria has diverse ecosystems, from savannahs and rainforests to deserts in the northern region.

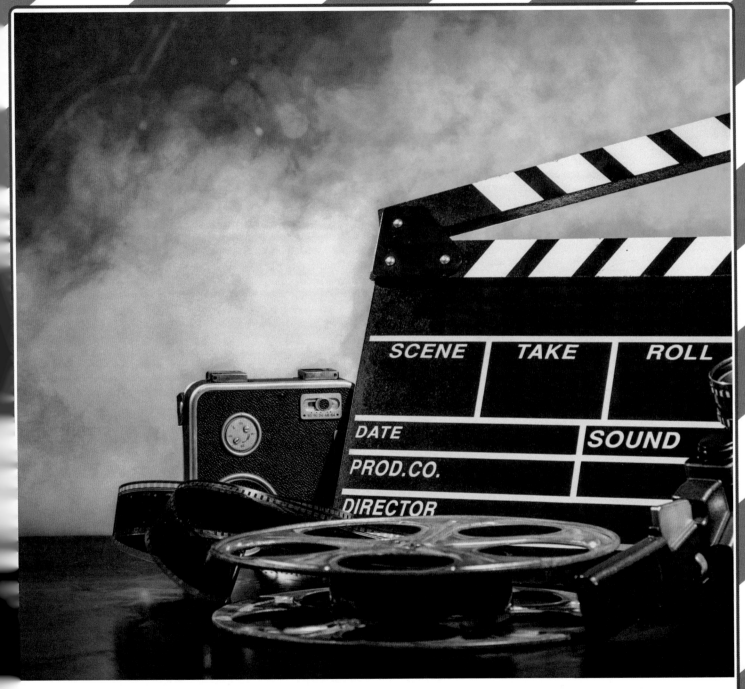

Nigeria's movie industry, Nollywood, produces thousands of films each year.

The Aso-Oke fabric is a traditional handwoven textile used for special occasions in Nigeria.

The Olumo Rock in Abeokuta is a popular tourist destination with historical significance.

Nigeria has a diverse range of traditional dance forms, each with
its unique cultural significance.

The Nigerian coat of arms features an eagle, a black shield, and colorful flowers representing the nation's diverse flora.

The Oshun-Osogbo Sacred Grove, a **UNESCO World Heritage Site, is** a sacred forest in Osogbo.

Nigeria has a significant diaspora community, with Nigerians living in various parts of the world.

The Lekki Conservation Centre in Lagos is a nature reserve and home to the longest canopy walkway in Africa.

Nigeria has a rich folklore tradition, with stories and myths passed down through generations.

The Yankari National Park in Bauchi State is home to a variety of wildlife, including elephants and baboons.

The Ogbunike Caves have 10 tunnels and various chambers, attracting both tourists and spiritual pilgrims.

The Durbar festival is a colorful event celebrated in several northern Nigerian cities, featuring parades and traditional horse riding.

Nigeria has a rich history, with ancient civilizations like the Nok dating back to 500 BC.

Nigeria is a member of the Commonwealth of Nations.

The country celebrates its Independence Day on October 1st with various events and festivities.

The Niger Delta, located in the southern part of Nigeria, is a major oil-producing region.

Nigeria has a space program and launched its first satellite, Nigeriasat-1, in 2003.

The Hadejia-Nguru Wetlands in Nigeria are essential for bird migration and conservation.

The traditional Nigerian attire for men is the agbada, while women often wear the gele headwrap.

Nigeria has a vibrant market culture, with popular markets like Onitsha Main Market and Kano City Market.

Butterfly bonanza: Over 1,300 fluttering species, Africa's richest haven for butterfly enthusiasts.

Nigeria has a growing tech industry, with cities like Lagos becoming hubs for innovation and entrepreneurship.

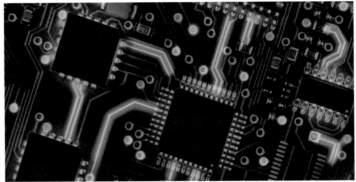

Nigeria has a diverse range of traditional festivals, such as the New Yam Festival and the Argungu Fishing Festival.

The Erin Ijesha Waterfall, also known as Olumirin Waterfall, is a natural wonder in Osun State.

TRAVEL TIPS FOR VISITING NIGERIA

1. **Plan Ahead:** Before traveling to Nigeria, make sure to research the places you want to visit, the local customs, and the necessary travel documents like visas and vaccinations.
2. **Stay Safe:** Nigeria is generally safe for tourists, but it's essential to stay vigilant, especially in crowded areas and at night. Keep your belongings secure and be cautious of your surroundings.
3. **Respect the Culture:** Nigeria has a rich and diverse culture, so it's important to respect local customs and traditions. Dress modestly, especially in religious or conservative areas, and ask for permission before taking photos of people or places.
4. **Stay Healthy:** Drink bottled water and eat food from reputable sources to avoid getting sick. Make sure to get any necessary vaccinations before your trip and carry a basic first aid kit with you.
5. **Use Reliable Transportation:** Public transportation in Nigeria can be crowded and unreliable, so consider hiring a private car or using reputable taxi services for getting around. Be prepared for traffic congestion in major cities like Lagos.
6. **Exchange Currency Wisely:** It's best to exchange your money at official currency exchange offices or banks to get the best rates. Avoid exchanging money with street vendors or unofficial sources.
7. **Learn Basic Phrases:** While many people in Nigeria speak English, learning a few basic phrases in the local language, such as Yoruba, Hausa, or Igbo, can help you communicate better and show respect for the culture.
8. **Be Prepared for Power Outages:** Nigeria experiences frequent power outages, so it's a good idea to carry a flashlight or portable charger with you. Some hotels and restaurants have backup generators, but it's always good to be prepared.
9. **Be Patient:** Things in Nigeria may not always go according to plan, so it's essential to be patient and flexible. Embrace the slower pace of life and take any delays or changes in stride.
10. **Enjoy the Experience:** Nigeria is a vibrant and exciting destination with a lot to offer, from bustling cities to beautiful natural landscapes. Take the time to immerse yourself in the local culture, try new foods, and explore everything this diverse country has to offer.

Made in the USA
Las Vegas, NV
03 October 2024

96225645R00026